ORAC

Poetry by James Harpur

A VISION OF COMETS
THE MONK'S DREAM

JAMES HARPUR

Oracle Bones

ANVIL PRESS POETRY

Published in 2001
by Anvil Press Poetry Ltd
Neptune House   70 Royal Hill   London SE10 8RF

Copyright © James Harpur 2001

This book is published with financial assistance
from The Arts Council of England

Designed and set in Monotype Bell by Anvil
Printed and bound in England
by Cromwell Press, Trowbridge, Wiltshire

ISBN 0 85646 325 6

A catalogue record for this book
is available from the British Library

The author's moral rights have been asserted in accordance
with the Copyright, Designs and Patents Act 1988

All rights reserved

Acknowledgements

A number of poems in the first section took their initial inspiration from *Divination and Oracles* (1981) edited by Michael Loewe and Carmen Blacker.

Poems in this collection have previously been published or accepted for publication in the following periodicals and anthologies: *Acumen, Agenda, New Exeter Book of Riddles, Other Poetry, Poetry London, PN Review, The Spectator, The Swansea Review, Temenos*.

The riddle 'With the dawn I arise' was broadcast on BBC local television; 'Chi Rho' is from a long poem, 'Voices of the Book of Kells', commissioned by the Poetry Society as part of their Poetry Places scheme; and 'Magna Karistia' was commissioned by the *Independent on Saturday*'s magazine for its millennium issue, 1 January 2000.

The author would like to thank Eveline O'Donovan, Anna Adams and Patrick Harpur for their help and encouragement and gratefully acknowledges the Society of Authors for a writer's bursary in 1999, and the director, administrator and staff of Hawthornden Castle for a fellowship in 1999.

Contents

PART ONE: *Oracle Bones*

'I stretch my arms'	11
Retired Augur	12
The Assyrian Extispicist	14
Letter to the Dead	17
Epiphany	19
Map in the Lake	20
Oracle Bones	22
The Hanging God	23
Cuchulainn's Fate	31
Oisín's Return	32
The Delphic Priest	35

PART TWO: *Journeying to Rome*

Nero's Deadline	47
The Gift of Prometheus	48
Divinity of Bees	49
Truth Lives Within Your Home	50
Journeying to Rome	51
Four Riddles	52
The Rose of Paradise	54
To His Wife	55
Pleasures' Stings	56
Fortune's Wheel	57
Anaximenes	58
Heraclitus	60
Portents	61
Impious Mars	62
The Great Animal Plague	63
Chi Rho	64

PART THREE: *Dies Irae*

Dies Irae 67
Magna Karistia 88
Cranborne Woods (17 May 1994) 91

PART ONE

Oracle Bones

Man's character is his daimon.
    HERACLITUS

*The man who submits to his fate calls it the will of God:
the man who puts up a hopeless and exhausting fight is
more apt to see the devil in it.*
    C. G. JUNG

*But the truth is that not a leaf falls from a branch without
cause, for to admit the power of chance in the physical
world is to detract from the power of the creator.*
    WILLIAM OF CANTERBURY

*Commit unto us thy eternal truth, O mighty turtle, that
we, by thy power, may be guided in our choice.*
    ANCIENT CHINESE INVOCATION

'I stretch my arms'

I stretch my arms like a swan flying
And watch, weightless, the world turning
So high up I can see – endlessly it seems
Rome and white mountains rising beyond,
Triremes at anchor in still Alexandria
Pearl-divers practising from rocks
The wind wandering through the wilderness.
The sun casts no shadow of the compass.
I am rooted to the spot, rotting inside
I had no choice but to choose this perch
And now I cannot choose any more
Each choice I made was like a nail
Fixing my arms to embrace the world.

Retired Augur

It is a matter of regret
I never had the confidence
To puncture the masks
Of taut anticipating faces.
Expectation fed my expectation
Or paralysed my anarchy.
I was too young and diffident
And to plunge my hand
In the stinging succulence
Clutch the slippery liver
And whip it out still steaming
With an ostentatious flourish
Had its own momentum
A fascination I once relished.

What made immortal gods
Pick out a clutch of dusty chickens
To cluck their messages
I never understood.
But the flight of starlings
Before the sun arose
Across a wintery sky
A mass of dotted light expanding
Contracting
The pattern always changing
Moment to moment
Yet held within the form
As a fishing net when swept
Above the sea
Poised in the liquid air
Unbuckles loosely –
Its lines of light and dark

Shifting in the sifting mesh
Then spreading in one glorious flow . . .
The point is beauty – not
Divine communication:
A flash of unprepared-for beauty
Penetrating, traceless
Before the mind can cast
Its predetermined meaning.

This world is moving into reason
The civil wars are over
Our hopes rest on triumphal arches
Staking culture from cold Britain
To the deserts of Judea.
Let bald fat-bellied Etruscans
Hawking crackpot superstitions
Piss away their lives in prophecy.
Let the rituals stagger on
As stabilising pageantry
But let us cease, cease
To crave the sphere of superstition.
Not gods, birds, sweating statues
But the manacles of law
The scourge . . . crucifixion
Shall usher in, ensure
A thousand years of peace.

The Assyrian Extispicist

The palace slides to darkness, sleep.
Corridors relieved of echoes.
A lion bellows at the moon.
I fidget, daydream, nip my nails
Anything but write reports.
Prophecy is mostly paperwork.
There are two roads on the liver.
The king will lead his men to Elam
Returning gloriously to Shamash.
The right lung has a tinge of red:
The king will bring his fire to Elam . . .
And so the future casts its shadow
And the king must have his certainty.

It was not a dream, exactly,
But I told the king in any case:
I saw him reclining in the garden
A table by his side, bowls of wine,
The queen was sitting opposite
Slaves wafting heat away with fans.
And from a tree-branch hung
The king of Elam's ragged head
Swinging gently on a rope
Like one thick grisly tendon.
And that I thought was that
The predictable event predicted.
But the tableau kept on moving
And this I could not tell the king:
He watched the head sway as he drank
Mesmerised, as by a mirror,
Somehow his wine had turned to blood

Had spattered round his turtle lips
And with every drop of blood he drank
His face grew paler, like a corpse.
And here I quickly stopped it.

These images were not from entrails
But came through living veins
Linking the tissue of the soul
With eyes of gods who watch our lives
With knowledge of their journeys' end.
There is imagination
That casts around for bric-a-brac
Selects and sorts, fossicks
Relies on stars and smoking offal
And passing thoughts to make a thing
Of uncompelling randomness.
There is imagination
That is insistent in its unity
Gives meaning to each particle
As cones of sunlight frame and gild
Every swirling speck of dust.
And there is also revelation
In which the future makes its entry
Like an unexpected guest
Or some outlandish foreigner
Full of tales and prodigies
From other worlds to come
Compelling our attention
For as long as we can hold it.
But that is only my opinion
And anyway the revelations
Do not always come to pass.
And anyway my job requires
The king does not know everything.

The liver has two fingers on the right . . .
Let me see . . . *The king will lead his men* —
No, I've done that one already.
Two rivals vie to seize the throne —
No, that needs some toning down.
Remember: keep it vague and simple.
Should truth emerge in clarity
Like a lion leaping from a stone
His body freed by finely chiselled lines
Then temper it with doubtful words.
Do not indulge imagination;
Above all, the king must be protected.

Letter to the Dead

Mother, where are you in the West?
Are stars as densely crushed as foam
Flung from the waterfalls of Nubia?
Do reeds grow thicker and higher
Than the columns of a temple?
Do you watch the river flood its banks
And ships draw in from distant oceans?
Is light composed of finer gold
Than at harvest time in Goshen?

This is your son who speaks to you.
I have brought you offerings
Of honey, wine and loaves of bread
At every sunrise since you left us
According to the ancient custom.
They say you live within a world
From where no one returns – I ask
That you appear just as you were
Before the sickness painted you
The colour of a ripened gourd.
I ask that you remove the dreams
That scuttle sideways through my sleep.
I chant the songs to this effect
And know that every fading sound
Sustains the particles of life.

Mother, where are you in the West?
Look down on those you left behind
And cure the numbing separation.
The threads that tied us to the gods
Are being severed like the sinews
Of a sacrificial goat

Tombs are cracked, spells destroyed
Church doors are locked on holy feasts
Sacred words fade from the columns.
Priests forget the meaning of the riddles
That fortified our dimming faith
And crocodiles grow lazy and obese
On the flesh of suicides.

Mother, where are you in the West?
Can you hear the songs I chant
Or do they fade to emptiness?
Appear to me, your hair well combed
Your hip and crooked feet now straight
Your eyes enjoying some small amusement.
Bring comfort in this time of darkness.

Epiphany

For twelve days the sky had been obscured.
The guiding patterns of the constellations
Lost behind a mesh of haze;
Our trackprints filled with sifting sand
Like a softly fading sequenced memory
Or the healing drift of doubtfulness.

Ascending to a ridge I saw the torchfires
Of Ctesiphon burn like streaming hair
And taken unawares was struck
By a sudden longing for my country, my people,
And such a pang for all things cherished
For the sunlit gardens of my childhood.

Releasing tears of deep relief – or grieving –
I heard the other two spontaneously
Humming a song of Zarathustra
As we slowly descended down the slope
Away from the dying vista of the future
Towards our past, closing in.

Map in the Lake

And so we came to the sacred lake –
A sea of solid salt below
A blur of hills that rose like ghosts,
Its thickened ice undamaged
Except there by the edge
A pool of water, black and shiny
Circled by an edge of ragged frost
A deepening mirror, waiting.
We sat, invoking stillness
Words humming like a prayer wheel
Padmasambhava, Padmasambhava,
The thousand voices struggled
Padmasambhava, Padmasambhava,
Dimmed and disappeared
Last flickerings of candle flames
Then like a shout the silence came
Skin and blood a tingling fusion
Skull and mind a membrane
A globe of sheer unearthly light.

In the splendour of the stillness
Images appeared from darkness
Touched the surface, almost shyly
Like deer emerging from a forest.
We watched the map fit into place
Assuming depth and clarity
To a sudden consummation –
Mountains rose above a valley
Workers bending in the barley fields
And closer in, a gilded temple

And running past it to the east
A sunlit road returning to a village
And there! a house with sea-blue tiles.

When we stepped inside
The young boy laughed
And clicked his tongue with joy.
He knew the names of each of us
And recognised my rosary.
We knew we had arrived at last
And remembered as a flash
The frozen lake, the still dark pool
And images scattering like fish.

Oracle Bones

The mountain pines are casting patterns.
In the stillness of the shade
A lion waits in dark green light.

The sun has bleached the shoulder blade.
Socket and nodules all removed.
The coals enrich the metal rod.
I drill out pouches from the bone
Blow dust away, wipe it smooth.
The future lies in preparation.

In dark green light a lion waits.
The mountain pines are casting patterns
In the stillness of the shade.

The knife-tip penetrates the blade.
I scratch, incise, engrave precisely
The necessary ritual words
To pin the shifting forces down:
The king will hunt successfully
Tomorrow in the afternoon?

In the stillness of the shade
A lion waits. In dark green light
The mountain pines are casting patterns.

And now the moment is in joint
Cosmic pressures
Tune together at this point –
A cracking from the hissing tip
Heat spits out a web of fissures
Towards the lion arrows rip.

The Hanging God

Beyond below the cliff the waves
Collapse to snowstorms, send seagulls
Spraying up in screams and claw
The shore and shingle rabidly
Suns rise, burn, set and rise again
To thin the blood inside my head
To glaze the leaking wound
Moons grow to chase their shadow selves
To find the aura of completion
The empty Wagon jolts around
The still, shining lake of north.

The world had circled round this ash
For five extinctions of the sun
When two bright stars became detached
Two watching eyes, they moved
Together through the static night
Until in measure with the dawning
Their light began to dim, grow dark
I saw they were two birds — ravens
Flapping and soaring alternately
And on they came in steady flight
And landed on my shoulder bones
Pressed nutshell-beaks inside my ears
Harder, tighter, pushed and forced
To birth pangs — my mouth a cave
Of mute release — a prisoner impaled —
They disappeared inside and when
The nausea had died my sight was cleansed —
Transfixed I saw with sharpened vision
The slow revolvings of creation
Through shadows of the circling sun

And in the darkness meteors
Ignite like flints and disappear
As fiery seconds into timelessness.
I saw across to other lands
Mountains blotched with snow and mud
Coils of riverlight below
And villages on empty moorland
Single travellers on roads.
I saw a city burning drunkenly
And, nearby, rows of sleeping bodies
Below the humps and stones of graveyards
All pointing to the rising sun;
I saw a man raised on a tree
I saw him clearly, magnified –
His eyes were incandescent coals
Grey-white and pink as coral
He looked at me, tried to speak
But words erupted from his mouth
In burning flickerings of green and blue
His body started belching gold
And smuts of ash that rose and grew
To birds with softly flaming feathers
Spiralling in a cone of fire
Then one split off and flew to me
I felt the blast-heat of its shadow
From the candle-mass of blaze
Its head was human, its face was young,
And beating at the air it spoke
In such a way there was no sound
And yet I heard the words as thoughts:

'You sought this sacred incubation
But now the sense of seeking stops
The subtle metamorphosis
From god to man, from man to god

And you will stay an inbetween
A soul in flesh, a god with blood,
Until you feel in every nerve
The body's moribundity
Repulsed by novel sights and sounds
And you cast off hollow memories
The future-tainting past, and face
Accretions of a life's neglect.'

With that it flew above my head
Turning back towards the sun
Changing dimensions
A silhouette of beating wings
A shadow flicking at the waves
It shrank, shrank and disappeared.

Nine days hanging on the ash
My body a charcoaled fish
My tongue a furry wedge of salt
The wound insinuating pain
From shins to teeth and as I hung
My bones pulled muscles further down
My lungs filled up with froth and filth
And from the woodbark of my skin
My past emerged, crept out
Discrete segmented sections
Slithering, virulent
Forgotten acts of treachery
Of cowardly indecisiveness
Sly words of implication
And out they crawled, and more
Uncongealing memories
Shivering, seeking air and light
Lingering on skin and membrane
Until I felt my mind retreating

Scratching the inside of my skull
The frenzy came and died – I slumped
A rag within a ragged frame
A morsel of the sun and wind and rain.

Nights and days arose and went
Thoughts coarsened into flesh
And flesh thickened into bone
A unity of numbness
A sagging lump of absence
But still I found I had the sight
Only sharper, more rarefied
I saw the composition of light
Glittering like a million silver flies
And every shining blade of grass
Distinct in every shade of green
And on the shore I saw strange stones
Gleaming from the dross of pebbles
Each one engraved with slight incisions
Like birdfeet, or small hooks or spears
And as the sea washed over them
They made grotesque growls
Above the gravel-gargling waves –
The noise of unframed speech that rose
In different grating grades of pitch
A chaos of cacophony –
No space between the dark vibrations
Intensifying in discordance –
I felt it forcing in sensation
And wedging me apart with noise
Until my body left my body:
In the image of the soul
It glided from its heavy frame –
One body hanging from the ash
The other under some instruction

Moved downward to the shore
Gathered up the gleaming stones
And standing near the creeping waves,
Screaming with ecstatic tension
Threw them high up in the air –
Spinning into chance or guidance
They landed – I looked, fell back
And instantly rejoined my flesh.
And from the tree I saw the stones
Had formed a pattern with a meaning
I could not understand – and yet
Their graven lines seemed interlinked
As if each needed all the others
For its single resolution –
Each sacrificed to make the whole.
And as the sea advanced, withdrew
Washing the configuration
I listened to the growls that turned
To chords of music, deep and steady
More resonant than beaten metal
Plaintive like the psalms of seals
Adjusting sounds, each to each,
Delaying individual notes
Then lifting gently, sweetly
Entwining in a harmony
Which stirred a recollection
Of somewhere else, another time
I could not quite recall –
I forced myself to grasp the memory
Then exhausted with the effort
I sank back further, withdrew
Within the honeycomb of music
Deeper, deeper until my mind
All purpose dissipated
Could only hear the notes

Conjoin to just one graceful tune
So pure in its intensity
It seemed to take a visual form –
A spot of light, a growing globe
Of silver, a sun behind a mist
A disk, a smooth shining mirror –
There! I saw myself spear-pierced
Slumped and haggard on the ash –
It was as if the universe
Had shrunk down to this brilliant eye
Staring, staring – I watched my face
Growing, staring back at me
Its mouth articulating words
Slowly and deliberately:

'You will not find the combination
Of meaning and its rightful music
By search and ingenuity
But by expecting nothing to occur.
Then out of depths of darkness ravens
Will fetch you words like twigs for nesting.
But some will come by other ways
By careless winds and waves: discard
Seductive oddities of flotsam
Fill your lungs with truth and speak
Until there's nothing more to say
Then let the holy silence come.
For words are only messengers
With cracked lips and dusty tongues
Forgetting slowly on their journeys
The messages they carry
From the author of creation.'

The light began to dim, the face,
And voice began to fade away

And on the shore I heard the stones
Break from their combination
Their music now diminishing
Below the waves returning harsher.
A wind began to shake the ash
And thoughts came crowding to my head
Like seagulls whirling round their screams
Or ghosts around a funeral ship
Demanding the blood of speech
I knew they were the thoughts
Of men and women, their prayers
To be acknowledged in their loneliness
To understand the reasons for
Their journey on the road to death;
Their hopes for finding love
Among the randomness of living;
Their aspirations to create
A personal immortality
Through flesh or wonderments of beauty;
Their need to celebrate the rapture
Of the oak tree in its massiveness –
A giant cranium of green stars –
And secret wish for sympathy
With all created life –
All humming to be cast in sound.
I felt the frailty of flesh
Unequal to the task of speech
The lack of solid boundaries
Not only with the living
But also with the long departed
As souls pressed in to speak
Searching for an incarnation
Of everything they had not said.
I knew this was the mission
The days and nights upon the tree

Had drained me of the will
To contradict necessity –
To articulate a dumb existence.
I did not have to search for words
I let all go and still was borne
Above the slowly moving earth
Half man, half god, obliged
To hang from mortal days
Dreaming of immortality.

Cuchulainn's Fate

When my slingshot failed to sink a seagull
On Baile's Strand a wingbeat brushed my soul.

When the cloakpin dropped and broke my skin
I saw a fountain spurting up to heaven.

When the Grey of Macha shirked his harness
His leaden hooves kicked heavy in my chest.

When weapons in my chariot clattered down
Thunder crumbled, rolled around my lungs.

When I ate the meat the three hags offered me
I chewed the sinews of my destiny.

And when the Washer at the Ford rinsed blood
From my shirt – I saw the salmon gulping red.

Each sign, a wounding – chance now purposeful
But there is beauty in the unavoidable

Fate cuts the web of her obliging favours
Bit by bit and I am freed from sacred law

So let taboo go and gnaw taboo to death
I blossom, growing in this fierce new breath

That fans my warlight as I face my foes
And if I die just say that I – I chose.

Oisín's Return

As soon as the jumbo jet
Began vibrating down
Through gruelling mist,
Broke into revelation –
Cars scattering in the wet
Like panicky mice
Fields in slushy greens
And people small as lice –
I filled up with regret.
But I was hounded by my fate.
My young wife Niamh
Had begged me not to go:
'Do not violate
The sanctity of innocence
The memory of your youth
In all its warm perfection.
The Ireland that you knew
Has changed beyond recall.
The past you take back with you
Will never recognize itself
But stumbling everywhere
Sniffing like a blind old dog
Will die of sweet remorse.
Listen to me! Do not trust
Your backward voice.
Stay here beside this sea
Where sunlight turns us gold
And time is open – here
Where nobody grows old
In glorious California.'

Thirty years of absence
Seemed more like three hundred.
Almu Street demolished
Tara Square rebuilt
The river where I fished
A gutter of slime and silt.
I drove out west to escape
Through shrunken lanes
To the Ballyhoura mountains
And cousins thrice removed.
I was a fool.
Hiking up a nearby hill
I watched two men attempt to shift
A six-foot slab of marble
Carved with *nouveau* Celtic script
'Here lies Oisín, the Fenian
Son of Finn McCumhail.'
They asked my help to lift it –
Distracted by my name
And by my father's name
Chiselled on the stone
I lent a dreamy hand:
Coordination went awry
I took the brunt
Staggered, slipped, collapsed
It landed on my front.
A busted rib cage, complications
Led to drips and scans
Intensive care.

The nightlight cools my tan
Dye is growing from my hair
Every ounce of flesh I lose
Adds pockets to my skin.
The priest keeps coming in

To see if I am well
With jokes about St Peter
At the gates of heaven
Directing heathen into hell.
In medicated dreams
I'm walking back from school
Through fields of waist-high grass
Towards the summer holidays;
I see my wolfhound stirring
And bounding to the gate;
Playing chess against my father
The heavy ivory pieces
My pleading to retract a move.
And I see the land of youth
Its shadowed light and blazing blue
Niamh swimming in the sea
Breaking through the surface
Like a golden seal.
Days and nights are fused.
My past is gone, and future too
All I am is present
Crept over, each day a year,
A slow paralysis
Leaving me two eyes
A memory in limbo
Cursed to stare
Into heaven or at paradise
Knowing wherever I go
That I am never there.

The Delphic Priest

My father's father's father said
That a long long time ago
When deities still came to earth
And mingled with the human race
The god of light appeared to us
One ordinary day in summer
Sailing from the blue across
The olive-shimmering sea
In a boat with shining sails
Disembarking on our shore
A veil of sun pinned to his face
His actions predetermined
By the slow revolving myth.
Below the sheer red Phaedriades
The snake lay sleeping in a coil
Guardian of a realm
Where undirected prophecy
Spilled like birdsong over fields
And time was undivided.
The snake saw in its dream
The figure marching through the glade
Of waves of startled olive trees
But saw too late the god's bright blade
Snapping to his command.

That was the story told to me.
Each place must have a myth to sing
To sanctify its crops and springs
And found its holy shrines
And this one blessed the ground of Delphi.
The princes, traders, craftsmen
Who made long journeys here

Driven or inspired by signs
From Ionia, the Cyclades
Along the stony wadis
Of Lydia and Lycia
Over Thracian plains and mountains
Or gliding through a copper sea –
These single-willed petitioners
Came to feel the living presence
Sought answers to unspoken questions:
Not, shall I move to Ephesus?
Nor, will my son regain his health?
But, is there some intelligence
Beyond the vacancy of temples?
They came to witness ecstasy
A brief irruption of the god
To slow down temporarily
The planet spinning in the head.

They came to seek out ritual
The reassurance of mystery
And stable certainty of fate.
As for me, the only ritual
That I can contemplate
Is getting out of bed each day.
Things have changed of late.
But still my memory kindles
The altar's hissing embers
The shivering sacrificial goat
Sharp fumes of laurel leaves
Ablutions in the icy stream . . .
For fifty years I have presided
Imagining behind the screen
The pythia with stiff nostrils
Inhaling foul mephitic steam
Deep within her rhythmic lungs

Her eyes whitening like seagull wings
A prayer half whispered, half sung
The rocking of the tripod
A flare of energy, a screech
A vomiting of god! god!
In spasms then growling speech . . .
It was bizarre how one could tell
The meaning of the utterance
How reason cracks
The ungorged burst of syllables
And renders it in syntax.
The god of light looks down on us.

Afterwards they often asked me
What on earth was going on
Some suspecting subterfuge
And I would look concerned and say:
In sleep our minds expand and reach
The universal realm of soul
Where fate spins out and weaves its threads
Of what has been and what will be
All present simultaneously
Where crossings of the woof and warp
Are nodal points of change
Of birth and love, decay and death
And fateful accidents
That give our lives their pattern.
The mind is saturated, charged
With knowledge of its destiny
The outcome of potential acts
Their endless causes and effects
Spiralling to infinity
Until it wakes and time and space
Obscure the sense of personal fate
And usher in the old routine

Of idiosyncracies and tics.
The oracle contrives release
From strictures of the intellect:
Apollo heals what he inflicts.
On the oak tree of Dodona
The dance of light that moves
Like the flick-flickering
Of eyes preceding ecstasy
And spills, tumbling leaf to leaf
As tremulous as wings of doves –
The watching self evaporates
And unifies with wind and tree
The circulating holy light
Seamlessly.

No one comes here any more.
The time of prophecy has passed
The signs withdrawn, the sun and moon
Glare down like sockets of a skull
And people seek an unseen god
Within their stinking godless selves.
No wonder that this shrine is sick.
A daily pilfering of stone
Encroaching lichen, weeds, rust
A coarsening of column lines.
Diminishing graffiti.
The pythia wheezes for breath
Her channels silting up with dust
Her dying living, a living death.

The rot had started years ago.
My father told me that his father
In the age of Constantine
One morning in the spring
Had seen a vision: out to sea,

A boat ablaze with sails of sun
As if a god were coming in;
A single figure stepped ashore
And in a nimbus of soft light
Glided through the swaying olives
Towards the Phaedriades.
At the bottom of the Sacred Way
He paused, his clothes and head
Pulsing a pearly sheeny rainbow
Changing to a flaming red
Then white the purity of snow.
He walked among the monuments
Mildly curious, half amused
Climbing to the temple.
Directly opposite the entrance
Three snakes appeared entwined as one
Reared up at him, spat and spat
Recoiled, shrank and then were gone
Never to be seen again.
And that was that.

I was reminded of the story
A month ago, the start of spring
Sirius crackling blue at night
Snowlines streaked on mountains
The dawn magnificent and crisp
I saw a ship approaching –
Its sail a wing of rose-red light –
At last some pilgrims!
I felt a stirring in my bones
As I watched the figures drawing near
Three of them, wealthy easterners
And hid my fears, anticipation
When I saw that they were courtiers
Brocade and smooth-white pampered hands –

Orientals bearing gifts.
The emperor wished to question god.
One blabbed about his master's dream
To resurrect the ancient rites
All grandiose new gleaming shrines
The honey reek of oxen blood
And noble priests and acolytes
Handsome, manly, fine white robes
Their spirits forged in holy fire.
In truth he caught me by surprise
I felt his feverish desire
The pulses of enthusiasm
Until I saw the chasm deepening
Darkening behind his eyes.

He knew that I knew that he knew
Our time had gone.
Futile to salt the rotten past.
From age to age new worlds are born
In relentless parturition –
Old priests like me might turn to tricks
To check the drift to impotence
To check the howls of vulpine prophets
Bursting with revelation
Meanwhile the new myth enters silently
In woods and subterranean streams
A whisper in the budding shoots
In voices, oracles and dreams
Then as in spring the snow
One dawning day has left Parnassus
In startling warmth of colour
A sudden spirit stirs abroad
Inaugurates itself
The cycle starts once more.

The emperor's men were children,
Wild-eyed and whooping
Climbing walls, shouting out inscriptions –
One, drinking from the Castalian,
Faked a comic trance, began
To spout his party-piece
In a strangled high-pitched voice
Until the cliffsides ran with echoes:

Ultima Cumaei venti iam carminis aetas;
Magnus ab integro saeclorum nascitur ordo.
Iam redit et Virgo, redeunt Saturnia regna;
Iam nova progenies caelo demittitur alto.

I forced a laugh, obligingly.
That night we drank three jugs of wine
The southeast wind began to blow
And one of them, quite maudlin
The one who loved astrology
With watery eyes and blackened tongue
Scrawled a question on a tablet
And handed it to me – I looked
And sighed and said I didn't know
But from the alcoholic trance
Words escaped and flowed despite myself
Like water springing from the earth:

We live in worlds in parallel
One measured by the changing day
Where shadows creep away from light
And sight ensnares desiring eyes
And reason tinkers with illusion
Until it dies from what it cannot see.
The other is insensible
But can be reached in sleep, the path

Winds through the sphere of dream
Where Proteus guards the gates and swaps
His shape from flame to snake to hare
And if you clutch his changing form
He lets you pass to Psyche's realm
Where fates are spinning destinies
And gods and daimons shuttle back
And forth to earthly groves and woods
Restlessly, torn between two worlds;
And passing through these milling forms
You penetrate the kingdom
Of ultimate creation – source
Of fire water earth and air –
A mountain rises, made of light
And at its centre, in a cavern
Its darkness brighter than the sun
The Lord resides, unmoved, in motion
A knot of flashing lightning frazzle
Dazzling outward, shimmering
In diminishing intensity;
Around him sprout or bubble
As from gradations of white light
The essences of life itself
Organic structures, abstract shapes
Forms of immaterial lines
Of pure vibrating light
Growing to perfection –
Circles, squares and octagons
Spheres, cubes and pyramids
Diamonds, starfish, honeycomb
A spider in its sticky web
Or rocks or mountain flowers
A fountain generating thoughts
Flung out like petals in the air
And fires of different heights and heats

The flames of lust, of spiritual love
Of purifying suffering
And all the vital essences
To which this world's phenomena
Aspire to grow in likeness –
All are dimly ascertained on earth
Through dream and deep imagination
Without the need of inbetweens;
Creation cannot stop itself
Its nature is to overflow
Communicating tirelessly
Through intervening realms
In filtered pieces, inklings
But rarely as a glorious whole –
An insight on a country walk
An intuition late at night
Fragments of a broken poem.
And people seek it all their lives
To end their separation
From its primordial light.
Prayer and meditation
Can penetrate the centre –
If faith supplies the energy
The channel is sustained
For guidance and for inspiration.

Next day I led them to the temple
To put the emperor's question.
The pythia had installed herself
An hour before we came to her.
She was a gentle woman
Hollow-eyed and almost toothless
Intense, consistent, with a flair
For timing, if not histrionics.
I handed in the tablet

And took my seat behind the curtain.
The smell of laurel tinged the air
But there was never any tension –
In seconds she was mumbling
Then loudly spat out gutturals –
I heard the meaning of the sounds
And quickly wrote it down as this:

'Inform the king the glorious temple
Has fallen into ruin.
Apollo has no roof above his head.
The bay leaves have no tongue
The speaking springs and streams are dead.'

They left at daybreak.
Sitting on a rock above the stream
Numbing my swollen ankles
I watched them trail away
Like the last words of a story.
Over by the threshing floor
The pythia was humming a song
And boiling some bones for our soup.
The sun burnt edges from a cloud
The early wind had dropped
And shadows from broken columns
Slowly shifted their position;
The world was turning round minutely
Without regret, without regard.
I briefly felt a surge of sorrow
Recovered, cupped water from the stream
Sipped it slowly
And waited for Apollo
To come to me for one last time.

PART TWO

Journeying to Rome

Nero's Deadline

Nero felt no inkling of anxiety
When the Delphic oracle warned him
To beware the age of seventy-three.
He still had lots of time for pleasure –
He was only thirty years of age.
God had given him ample leisure
To handle hazards yet to come.

And now he will return to Rome
Feeling somewhat tired
But a lovely glowing tiredness from
A journey full of self-indulgent days:
Sporting contests, gardens, plays
Evenings in Achaian cities –
Above all else, the joy of naked bodies.
That's what Nero thought.

Meanwhile in Spain, Galba secretly
Musters troops and trains them – and he
An old man who is seventy-three.

FROM THE GREEK OF CAVAFY

The Gift of Prometheus

And I revealed the many different types
Of divination – I was the first to forecast
From dreams what has to happen in the future.
I showed how omens are interpreted
From people's words heard seemingly by chance
Or from a sign encountered on a journey.
I pointed out the flight of birds of prey
And which are sinister or bring good luck
Explaining all their quirks and various habits
As when they squabble, play or sit together.
I showed how smooth their entrails had to be
What colour gods will look for in the gall
The speckles found on healthy liver-lobes.
I burnt thigh- and back-bones wrapped in fat
Teaching men this esoteric art.
And as for seeing portents in a fire
I opened up their long-benighted eyes.

AESCHYLUS: *Prometheus Bound,* 484–499

Divinity of Bees

From all this evidence some people say
Bees share in the divine intelligence
And have imbibed the heavenly ether.
For God, they say, pervades all things:
The land, vast oceans and the endless skies.
Flocks and cattle, man and beast, draw in
The subtle breath of life from God when born.
Eventually all things return to him
And in their dissolution are absorbed.
For death does not exist: alive all rise
To heaven and the company of stars.

VIRGIL: *Georgics* 4, 219–227

Truth Lives Within Your Home

I chuckle when I think a fish immersed
In water has a need to quench its thirst.

Don't you see – your hearth is where God reigns
And not those woods you journey to in vain.

Truth lives within your home. Seek out Mathura
Or set off to Benares . . . or wherever:

Unless you make your soul a welcome guest
No place on earth will let you take your rest.

AFTER TAGORE'S *Songs of Kabir*, XLII

Journeying to Rome

There is a heavy toll
Involved in journeying to Rome
And very little gain.

The king you wish to find in Rome
You'll seek and seek in vain
Unless he travels in your soul.

AFTER THE IRISH, 8TH CENTURY

Four Riddles

1

I work in the evening, alone and in silence
My book's always open all the year round
I redeem the blankness, embellish white space
Press gold onto leaves, gilding the edges.
I crimson the plush of curling roses
And ring with corn-light the crowns of pilgrims.
As darkness approaches I dash off last rubrics
Wash out my brush in reddening water
Sink into bed and snuff out my lantern.

2

With the dawn I arise, but die in the night
My body feeds on the flowing of light
My shadow's cast from my shining soul
A pool of amethyst, pearl and gold.

3

Pale as a mist, I appear in the ocean
A ghost on black waves against moonless skies.
Some say I bring luck, some a misfortune.
My pennants stream back, my sail is round
My cargo is frozen but defies a great heat.

I journey alone along the same bearing
Steering past icebergs and islands of silver
Seeking the One, the world's golden glory.
When I have seen it I slip back to darkness:
The vision compels me to keep on returning.

4

A thought – I saw it! – silver and darting
Out of the blue – a blink and gone
A streaking fish – scratch of light.

The Rose of Paradise

So, manifested as a pure white rose
    Appeared to me the holy band of souls
    For whom Christ shed his blood to make his spouse.
As for the other sacred host – the angels
    Who while they're flying watch and hail the splendour
    Of the One who wraps them in love's folds
And praise the goodness that informs their nature –
    Like a swarm of bees who sip from petals
    And then rejoin their hive to turn their labour
Into the sweetest honey, so these angels
    Alighted on this flower's layered crown
    Then flew up high to where their love's immortal.
Like softly flickering flames their faces shone
    Their gold-winged bodies dazzled more than snow
    And as in serried ranks they landed on
The rose they radiated peace – the glow
    Of love their whirring wings absorbed in flight.
    Teeming between the heavens and the rose
They did not block the glory or the sight
    Because the light of the divine spreads through
    The universe according to its rights
And nothing can prevent it doing so.

DANTE: *Paradiso* XXXI, 1–25

To His Wife

Let us live, dear wife, as we have lived
And call each other by those names that lingered
On our lips the first night of our love.
As years add wrinkles to our ageing skin
I hope to God the day does not arrive
When I forget you are my sweet young thing
Or you no longer see me as your suitor.
Though you outlive the prophetess of Cumae
And I surpass the age of old King Nestor
This ripe longevity we shall deny:
Instead of ticking off the days of life
We'll count the joys they bring, my dearest wife.

AUSONIUS: *'Uxor vivamus...'*

Pleasures' Stings

All pleasures have the same capacity
To spur you on but leave you hankering.

Like bees who've poured out honey, pleasures flee
And leave their stings inside you festering.

BOETHIUS: *De Consolatione* 3, 7:1–6

Fortune's Wheel

Fortune turns her wheel as wilfully
As water surging in and out of creeks.
She crushes once-feared monarchs callously

Raises the vanquished . . . but only for a while.
She's deaf to cries, untouched by human grief;
The groaning she provokes just makes her smile.

It's her hobby! – how she proves her power
Impressing us with her great party trick
Of conjuring tears from joy within an hour.

BOETHIUS: *De Consolatione* 2, 1:1–9

Anaximenes

Our souls are air, just watch the breath
That enters icy, reappears
A curling ghost on early morning walks
Through groves of pines that stretch
Along the hills above the sleeping town.

As below, so above. One winter when
Shrubs shrank in naked tangles
Oaks and beeches, flashing willows
Let light glide through bare branches;
When grass subsided, bushes melted
And the forest opened up its paths
Like channels clearing after meditation
When the shrouded sun stood still
I suddenly saw the vision –
Creation as an uncreated movement
The *pneuma* in a never-ending stream
Of infinite mobility and tenderness
Assuming ever-fresher forms,
A light that loses nothing from itself
Materializing in the world
And shifting like a swarm of bees
To shape new particles of meaning:
Air was thickening into mist
Then slowly coarsened into rain
Which gathered friction, splashed
In ruts and filled up pools
Grew denser into slush and mud
That time would harden into stone
Or turn by rarefaction back to mist
To rise up thinning into air again
Then growing rarer still –

Refining and refining further
Into flickering grains of flame
Streaming up in sparklings
To coalesce in fiery pools to shine
From the hemisphere of darkness
As stars and moon and sun.

Heraclitus

A winter's day is ringing after rain.
Doves bedazzled in the walnut tree
My garden flowers drip with silver
Beyond, the fields are slashed with mercury
As if a star had dropped from outer space
Impacting into streaks of wobbling light;
With fireflies the hedges flicker
And gritty rutted tracks up-spurt sparks.

My soul is fiery aether, and stares
From mediating flesh, translucent eyes
In rapture at the shorn transfigured land
In sympathy, like with like,
At nights so dark the stars recede to bort;
Flaring, a mystery to itself, a dove
Erupting into snowy flames.

Portents

It was then that inauspicious filaments
Kept turning up in pessimistic entrails;
Blood flowed from wells, hilltop cities echoed
As wolves let off their howls throughout the night.
Clear skies had never witnessed so much lightning
Nor nights so many apocalyptic comets.
Again at Philippi two Roman armies
Fought each other with their Roman weapons.
Nor did the gods consider it an outrage
That Roman blood should fertilize again
Emathia and the rolling plains of Haemus.
The time will surely come in those domains
When farmers ploughing up their fields will jar
Their ploughs on spears decayed by leprous rust
Or clunk their hoes on empty helmets, gasping
When graves disgorge the giant bones of heroes.

VIRGIL: *Georgics* 1, 483–497

Impious Mars

Here, where right is wrong, and wrong is right
So many wars flare up across the world –
All sorts of outrage everywhere . . . ploughing
Does not receive the honour it deserves
With farmers called to fight the fields grow tatty
And sickles are hammered into rigid swords.
There's war in Parthia, war in Germany;
And having broken their alliances
Neighbouring towns are at each others' throats:
Impious Mars careers across the globe
As when the chariots surge from their stalls
And rattling round and round the track the driver
Clenching his reins to no avail is swept
Along by horses heedless of his tugging.

VIRGIL: *Georgics* 1, 505–514

The Great Animal Plague

Released from hell, from darkness into daylight
Ghost-white Tisiphone the Fury raged
Spurring on fear and sickness; every day
She raised her ravening head up even higher;
Parched river banks and hills repelled the baaing
Of sheep and endless bellowing of cows;
She cut down animals in swathes and heaped
Their foul corrupted corpses in their pens
Till people learned to dump them in a pit
And seal it up with earth: the hides were useless –
No one could get the flesh scrubbed up with water
Or transform it with fire; no one could shear
The fleece – so messed it was with filthy sores –
Nor touch the rotten threads spread on the loom;
And if you could put on that vile material
Raw boils and rancid sweat would spread along
Your putrid limbs and soon that blasted fire
Was eating up your sickness-ravaged body.

VIRGIL: *Georgics 3, 551–566*

Chi Rho

FROM 'VOICES OF THE BOOK OF KELLS'

How can we sentence the etherial
To the inertia of a pigment
And can the incorruptible
Be rendered in corrupt material –
And so on. Just further questions
Tossed in to keep the mind from sinking
In the sucking bog of detail
It madly yearns to drown in.
Excuses scurry to their holes
Procrastination pleads with me
Doodling an otter in the margin.
One chance to paint eternity
To consummate my begging talent –
But how can God be mediated!
He shines in every wave that breaks
From formlessness to formlessness.
How can I cage the glory?
Stay within the frame, concentrate
Let inspiration blow; freewheel
Unravel ingenuity
Be selfless in this holy work
Unknown to man but loved by God
For every single cherished stroke.
Dip the brush and let it rove
Invest your faith in it, and go
Into the unknown waiting void –
Just make the start, the rest will flow:
First the Chi, and then the Rho.

PART THREE

Dies Irae

In every moment slumbers the possibility of its being the eschatological moment: you must awaken it.

RUDOLF BULTMANN

The day of the righteous king
The day of the Lord is coming
The day of revenge and anger
Of darkness and miasma
The day of shocking wonders
The day of shattering thunder
The day of tightening fear
Of bitterness and tears
When love of women ceases
Desire gives way to peace
When the urge to fight has flown
And worldy lust has gone

FROM THE 'ALTUS PROSATOR',
ATTRIBUTED TO ST COLUMBA

Dies Irae

And willingly, unwillingly
Every moment of our lives
We draw closer to the end –
Once again it is returning
The doors are open, no one comes
Once more I face the vast expanse
A pigeon flutters round a capital
I know I have to speak
But words are wrapped in webs of thought
And nobody is here to hear me
I know I know this strange basilica
The light is darker in the windows
Than in the distant corners
There is the presence of a multitude
But nobody is here – that's right
And then I have the thought:
Don't they know that I can save them?
And then I think: what is this emptiness
And why is it so hot
I know I shouldn't be here
There is the presence of a darkness
Or absence of the light
Jesus, pity me a sinner
Jesus, pity me a sinner
The shadows shift like spiders
Jesus take me out of here –
Stay calm, stay calm
You're only in your room
These are your walls, this is your bed.
The time has not yet come.

The cracked glass lets out the heat
Sounds flow in as funeral noise
A sheep crying like a woman
Its imprecations hacking God
Bonfires spitting in the street
Stillness, a sultry curfew
A shout – flap of running sandals
Nervous whistling from the guard.
The signs are here –
Last week the moon a blood-sac
Angels slinging javelins of light
Across the slatey firmament
Jesus I must sound the warning!
Keep calm. Breathe deep
Keep calm, isolate an image . . .
Sunlight skimming off the waves
The cutting shadow of a sundial
The cypresses of Syracuse
Concentrate, concentrate
Oxen working on the fields
An evening clearing out its rain
The golden slopes of Etna
Massive, pregnant, still
Oxen winding up and down
Uncovering a wine-dark tilth
Every row a wake
Of shining transformation
Wheeling round, up and down
Unravelling time
Until the field is finished
The final revelation.

This mansion wheezes in the dust
Walls flake off dead skin
The air is thick with stifled hope

This bed my diocese
Of fevered ambition.
Time is running out.
How can I save a single soul
When all I think about is hell
Scythian winds freeze me
The Dog Star burns me dry
The cycles gain more virulence.
Jesus, help me
Drive me on before it's time.

The sheets are drying out
Thoughts untwisting from the heat
I cannot rest, I must have rest –
Not yet, you must rehearse the words
Look, they shuffle through the doors
As white as geese
Disorientated, panic-stricken
They peer around the columns
And more and more of them
Flowing through the glarelight
Pressing, coughing, waiting
In a smoke of whispers
Scatter the atoms of each word
Like sparks of light
Upon their heavy bodies
Your spirit will be stifled
By any hesitation
Float above your crippled flesh
And do not think, just speak –
Our ship begins to leave the port
Cuts through the open sea to start
Its voyage to a far-off land.
Oblivious of choices
It progresses undeflected

And willingly, unwillingly
Every moment of our lives
We draw closer to the end . . .

Why would they listen to a voice
Repeating repetitions
Dropping words like dirty coins
Into a dried-up well?
Let them feed on comets
Misshapen foetuses and birds –
No! They wait for you to speak
One phrase could separate
Heaven from damnation
Engorge their cold imaginations
Make it happen in their eyes
The morning flops to darkness
And phosphorescent stars
Swim out of clouds in shoals
Hymns vibrate among the tombs
The watermills stop clacking
And through the windows lampfires flare
Like souls exploding with joy
A nauseous whispering
A million tiny whirring wings
Hollowing the body
Nerves excruciated
Every hackle delicate
And whoosh! the curtain blown apart
By holy fire the mind turned inside out
And all is light and light
Created like another body
And God is all around you –
Your life has hungered for this day
Has lived the present back from it
Revelling in finality

For endings bless the sequence
Give point and certainty
To everything that goes before
To stop the drift of being
And death by pointlessness:
You must prepare them for it –
I can't – they're too absorbed in flesh
They have no aim but now,
Inching on like ghostly arrows
In spaces equal to themselves
They think the end will never come.

More gather in the crush
Dampish body heat and breath
White window-sheets of light
Flooding the interior, a rush
Of expectation like a wind
What will I say to them? –
You must perfect each word –
But nothing can be adequate
The truth grows coarse articulated –
But you are all they have – start
And it completes itself
Your words shall flow as sunlight
Breaking on their faces
Take heart, breathe deep
The process will protract your speech
They have a single chance
To reach the company of saints
Redemption cannot be deferred
Each fraction of each moment
Decides our death eternally
No second must be wasted . . .
Make them see the dance of worlds
Reborn from fire endlessly

Is a mirage of revivalists
Who dream through golden glass
Of constellations sliding stars
Reduplicating ancient patterns
Planets synchronising as before
Necessitating new events
Exactly as they were before:
A cycle cannot be saved
From its seamless circularity
As myth will sink below
The flood of its own timelessness
But history is the ladder of the soul
Ascending and descending
Connecting earth with heaven
Conferring points of purpose
With one last crowning act –
Without the coming day
There can be no salvation
It is the shock and shattering
That keeps our lives intact.

Within this dripping corpse
I cannot muster any meaning
Phrases buzz around my head
Irritating bits of skin
Shoot off then flop, lie still and die –
Keep imagining the urgency
And let the detail come –
Last week I saw a blood-red moon
Last week a bloody moon –
Concentrate, concentrate –
Last week a bloated bloody moon
The giant face of Mars
Rose slowly from the seventh hill
At night the fields and rivers flare

With fallen stars
And from the north barbarians
Roll slowly down like rancid wind
Last night the sound of marching men
Became a roar of rushing waters . . .

Don't stop, keep practising
How long before it comes again
And pins you like a lizard
To a burning rock
And reason melts away in heat
And lets you churn in hell –
I cannot formulate new thought
It is as much as I can do
To reach in for my prayers
And keep the circles of the psalms
Turning and returning
To break the demons of the night
Who gather round my bed
With faces of forgotten friends
Or faces of the dead
Their eyes like distant candle flames
Waiting for a chink of doubt
The smallest breach of faith
A slip of reason. *When I say*
My bed shall give me comfort
You frighten me with dreams.
You terrify me with visions.

Like that one some days ago.
I woke up with a jump and felt
A presence in the room
A smell of wax and incense
And then I saw the silhouette
Hooded, kneeling by the window

Arms horizontal
I screamed to wake the dead
But only heard a muted yelp
And then I woke again and watched him
Stand up and move towards the bed
I felt my lips
Murder the creed
His face came close to mine
Somehow the light had been reversed
His skin was black, his pupils brown
His nostril hairs silvery
His pearly irises intense
And as we stared I heard him say:
'There was no defining moment
That made you kill me years ago
An accumulation of decisions
Mostly small and unconsidered
Or so it must have seemed
Each one you justified by each
And then one day the deed was done
My life's meaning, my life's blood
My sense of inner constancy
From silent prayer, the riches from
The moments in the cloister
Afternoons of summer heat
When the white layers of meditation
Would expand, rise and interleaf
With firmament on firmament –
All this you drained to death
And turned it into personal power
And you never even noticed
But still you cannot exorcise
The voice that calls you to the desert
Cannot ignore the crucifix's eyes
That widen as you fall asleep

Each night you look beneath your bed
And blast with shouts your silent dreams
Reminding you of solitude
Until the morning re-engraves your mask
With all the lines of certainty –
The high priest of salvation
And messianic theatre:
You think that when the day arrives
And he returns on clouds of fire
His face will look like yours.'
He turned his back and moved away
Rejoined the dark interior
And left me there, a lump of flesh
My bed a tomb, sheet a shroud
Waiting for the fever to abate
Confessing all my sins aloud.

But I was forced to take this path
My body is my witness –
Each night it begged my soul to heal
The wounds my will inflicted on it
The corn doles, and ordnance
Letters of diplomacy
Letters of encouragement
Battle plans, maps, sketches
I had to do it all myself
And all the while I watched
The *via contemplativa* stretch
From cloister to the garden
And out through snowy apple trees
The bristling greenery of fields
Running like a river's silver threads
Through valleys of repose
Around the distant hills
To paradise. I never chose this life

God chose it for me, and the sign
He sent was crowd hysteria –
He knew I'd have to take control
And I was desperate for a portent
My eyes alert for prodigies
To trigger what I knew deep down –
What else can differentiate
Between the will of God or self –
What else? No argument or reasoning
Can drive you to a monastery
A hermitage, or papal throne.

But I never knew what sign or voice
Drove her to withdraw from life
And seek out solace in that cell
Beyond the touch of human warmth
One glimmering plaque of light
To remind her of eternity
Her sole companions
A silver cross my father bought her
For their wedding anniversary
A copy of the psalter
Elongating widowhood
Self-inflicted innocence.
When I saw her rounded face
Reduced to holy angles
Her matted tufty hair
And fluid sympathising eyes
Become a hermit's stare
I could have sworn at God
Within the clammy silence
But tried to marvel at her chosen fate
Withheld the urge to speak
To hold her gently in my arms
Not wanting to disrupt her peace

Not wanting to interrogate
God's providence.
Then when I turned to go
She turned to me and whispered
I am exhausted crying out for help
My throat is dry, my eyes are dim
Through looking for the Lord.
We do not see the signs
We have no seers any more
And no one knows how long.
I held her, felt her arms
Hang down like bits of rope
And left, carefully shut the door
And trudging in the dusk
Watched her in the distance
Brushing strands of light
Into her long untangling hair
Rippling, flowing free
In the mirror of her bedroom
Two windows side by side
Letting in the summer sky
In eyes of lapis lazuli.

Do not relapse to sentiment.
Soft memories sap the will
Your mind and spirit must be rigid
With the presence of intention
Your duty is sacrosanct!
How can you lie and watch
The world revolving round you
In stealthy bars of gold and shade
While day by day it falls apart
Swarms of flies in water troughs
Prayers spoken scruffily
The wind so dirty – stir yourself! –

I do, I try, I strain
To hold it all together
Within my trained imagination
I bring the dead to life
I fortify the walls and gates
I feed the poor with bread:
Nothing is destroyed
If pictured long and hard enough;
Eternity is ringed
Within my mind and soul
I hold the universe inside
Then servants break the spell
And fill their void by feeding me
With scraps of hell
The starving fatten in the gutter
Soldiers sell off friends as slaves
Women sell themselves for meat
Dogs scratch up new graves
And worse: senators and priests
Spat at, stoned and cursed —
Then you must save their souls!
The starving must obey the law
The dying must obey the law
Challenging authority
Condemns them all to burn.

Begin by making them recall
That day of high dementing sun
Clouds foaming with the heat
Light made visible by dust
Rising from the distant plains
And how they lined the wall
As motionless as effigies
Transfixed by the parade
Devils with long shaggy hair

Curtaining their faces
Pulling laughs like horses
Prodding lines of citizens
Chained neck to neck
Some with stumps for hands
Some blinded, bawling like lambs
Or hopping forwards on one leg
And as the memory returns
Ensure they see that hell is chaos
Disjunctive violence
The blind hacking the blind
In mutual random mutilation
Milling senselessly around
Frenzied by their lack of purpose
Except the frenzy for killing;
Then say the only hope is structure
The sacred hierarchy
The martyrs, saints and angels
And archangels rank by rank
Arranged around the Lamb.
Salvation is the patterning of heaven
We must impose on earth.
Rulers rule, slaves slave
Self-knowledge is to know your station –
I know I am the servant of the Lord
I am the servant of the Lord
I am the servant of God's servants . . .

You are the first because you are the last:
Stiffen your mind, stiffen your body
Your mission has not finished –
But I can barely breathe this fleshy air –
But you can think and visualise
And God will give you sustenance
Look, they wait for you to rise

They peer around the columns
Pressing in to hear your words
A flame gathers on your tongue
A rose of crinkling fire
Each syllable igniting
Inside their passive heads –
I need more time to formulate
To make the last the perfect –
Time expands your hesitations
Perfection comes with God alone
Do not think about his spirit
But trust it to inform your tongue
And love the imperfections –
I have no lungs to pump out words
A cracked voice in creaking bones
Mocking the stentorian silence –
You sealed a covenant with God
To save as many as you can
Your sole excuse can be your death
They are waiting for you
Coughs and whisperings secede
To ravenous expectation –
What will I say, how shall I start . . .
The day is near, where will you run
Away from bears to jackals?
Or pant inside a cave to find
Your eyes adjust to coils of snakes?
Your faces smirk in mock disgust
But even in this hallowed space
Some flush with hot degrading lust
I see demonic spiders scrabbling
On arms, necks, whispering into ears
Darkening the light of sympathy –
Be temperate, speak steadily

Eschew sensation and its rhetoric
Develop meaning through its image
Let form cohere with matter —
Our ship begins to leave the port
Cuts through the open sea to start
Its voyage to a far-off land
And willingly, unwillingly
Every moment of our lives
We draw closer to the end . . .

But surely now it's all too late.
The time for understanding finishes
And now the burning must begin.
The meaning of each word lies in
The shortfall of its meaning
Where what remains is truth
Untranslateable in sound
But lying there where sound has died
Beyond the deadening yellow parchment
Of sermons, prayers and letters.
All my life I've scattered words
Like seeds on frozen ground
Rattled by winds from place to place
Scampering like hailstones
Unpenetrating, unpersuasive.
Have words changed anything
Except the beauty of a silence? —
Your putrid flesh infects your mind
Don't judge your language by response
The Lord speaks in your words not through them
The meaning disappears within
The surreptitious music
Sanctified despite itself
As wine can be transformed from wine

By whisperings of holiness
From tainted tongues of tainted priests.

And words are all I have to nurture
Wifeless, childless . . . almost witless
Feeding and sustaining them
Inside the black ark of my head –
How can I prepare the world
For the great winnowing
With coupling nouns and adjectives
Rhetorical questions?
I marvel how it came to be
That God gave me his favour
I who was to be a bureaucrat
From the age of four – at most
A minor statesman or a diplomat.
Perhaps he liked the isolation
A childhood framed by grammar
Miasma of studium
Oozing through the heavy house
My father always taciturn
Escaping life within his room
Except that once, that summer evening
Some fifty years ago – or more
Sitting in the garden
Struggling with a point of law
I gazed across the roofs
Stretching below the garden wall
To the empty line that marked the river
To hills, distracted clouds
Listening to the rattling carts
Stillness in between the shouts.
Beneath the nearby sycamore
My father sat with paperwork

His tidy beard bobbed gently
In rhythm with his silent reading.
He glanced at me, pulled up sharp
To address the panorama.
United we surveyed the city
Spread out like an audience
And then the distant clouds broke
A waterfall of hazy light
Cascaded in a golden fan
And rolled a wave towards us
Roof by roof – it struck our waiting house
And all the windows in a blaze
Of shining shields of bronze –
My father blurted, almost sang
My soul lives and shall praise you
Then smiled at me, returned to work
And stopped, looked up, and smiled again
I felt lightened, lifted, blessed
Embarrassed by my longing for affection.

Father help me in this hour
It comes again to test me
Again this subtle separation
Of flesh and bone, blood and brain
The temperature is rising
The wind so dense and stale
And I am growing colder
O crystalline Jerusalem
Remain pristine within my life
The city lessens with each shock of wind
Columns crumble like old vertebrae
Haphazard tiles cascade and smash
Dry fountains fume with excrement
Will no one clean me of this ordure?

They steal my books and letters
To fuel the funeral pyres
Aqueducts are dripping off
A thousand years of law and order
My waterjug is empty
Are all my servants still asleep?
Can no one hear my shouts . . .
Will no one stay awake with me?
The windows let in darkness
The world descends to darkness —
Stay calm, you must have faith
The city does not need the sun
The city does not need the moon
The glory of the Lord gives light to it
And the Lamb its lamp . . .

Stay calm, you must have faith
You must begin the letting go
You have accomplished all you could
And your journey shall be smooth
From this world to the other
A beautiful extinction
The dying of the flames of need
The rubbish of ambition burnt
The weight of aspiration lifted
Like that day so long ago
When you were sitting in the cloister
An afternoon of summer heat
The columned shade across the stone
The light, hazy and beneficent
Every slightest sound distinct
And every slightest movement
Relaxing in your vision . . .
I was alert, my mind was still

But questing farther, farther
Beyond the margin of the will
Until I had no will to turn
But revelled in a realm dissolved
Of doubt, a mist of hovering light
Created from my skin
And all the while my body lost
Its pressing weight of gravity
Floating on a sea of light
Until it was a sea of silvering light
Contained but uncontained
Easing in a fine contentment
And then the Silence came
A thunderflash that broke
The clinging fibres of resistance
Blanching all distinctions
Turning flesh to spirit –
Arms and legs were beams of sun
Extending from a glorious core
Of endless still but mobile light
Streaming from the fountainhead
Of solar light
Nothing more was left, no time no space
Just a unity
Of consciousness of consciousness
Purity, purity

And joy released from every pore.

At last it is approaching
The glory leaves the darkened temple
Embers of the stars have died
I am a brother of the jackals

And here I am again inside
This vast and empty space
The ceiling like a vault of shadow
The windows dusty tapestries
And no one here to hear me
Dumb before the emptiness
It all seems so familiar
Darkness turned to grey
Brightness turned to grey
Is this the vacant mind of God
I know I have been here before
I could not move until I spoke
I cannot speak until I think
And thought repeats my life
In thought my life repeats itself
Jesus, pity me a sinner
Jesus, pity me a sinner

Let go, don't hesitate
Leave thought behind you in the flesh
And say what must be said
Look, they've come to hear you speak
And not the ones you were expecting
These people come to welcome you
The doors are opening to light
And they are flowing through them
They come to welcome you
Flowing through the open doors
Refreshed and clothed in white
The windows glint like distant stars
Tall columns glowing like the moon
And altars golden as the sun
And every word you had to speak
But never had the chance to say

Can now be said – so rise and speak
Rejoice in your irrelevance
They wait in crowded joyfulness
Look – there's your mother, smiling
She looks so young and bright
Radiant in her primal form
She wants to speak to you
And there beside her is your father
Looking all around with awe
Laughing, marvelling at this great basilica
So bring an ending to it all
Discharge the warped rehearsals of your life
And join the happy company
What were you going to say? –
It does not matter now
Thought replaces speech
And grace replaces thought
Needlessly communicating
Freely and abundantly
Eye to eye, heart to heart
And so I leave my words behind
In memory of my self
And start again, to live another life –

Our ship begins to leave the port
Cuts through the open sea to start
Its voyage to a far-off land.
On deck or in the hold
We talk, listen to our thoughts
Write letters, sleep or walk about
Watch the sun skimming the waves
At night the phosphorescent stars
Swimming from underwater clouds.
Each fraction of each moment,

We choose to act, or think we do,
Yet all this time the ship advances
A solid vessel on its course
Indifferent to predicaments
Oblivious of choices
Progressing undeflected
And willingly, unwillingly
Every moment of our lives
We draw closer to the end.

Magna Karistia

I leave parchment to continue this work, if perchance any man survive and any of the race of Adam escape this pestilence and carry on the work which I have begun.
— FRIAR JOHN CLYN, KILKENNY, 1349

Lord, your work is now reversed.
No cockcrows spit out the bloody dawn
Wheat whispers like fields of glittering wasps
The fruits of orchards hang down
Fat and untested . . . we crumble to the dust
From which we were once born.

How can all this dying bring redemption?
How will you burn us into angels
With skin of gold of the light of sun
From blackened bodies dumped in wells?
Forgive my doubts of heaven
Amid the sweet miasma of this hell.

Who will survive to shoot memories
From age to age like swallows
Joining distant countries?
Who will preserve fire, earth, snow
The first green shivering of trees
The flow of pilgrims to the Barrow?

The reason that you made us —
Surely — was to witness your creation?
Without us what will be your purpose
As you walk around your garden
In eardrum-silence, echoes
Of the hooves of Death spreading on

And on – each night my sleep is beating
Over what my being has amounted to
Beyond cold vigils, chanting,
The isolation of beatitude
Always giving thanks and never doubting
Why so much of it was due.

I gave my youth to find your paradise
Within this cell and cloister
Now every little sacrifice
Flares and rages – has stripped me to a pair
Of jittery fiery eyes
Skidding off corpses everywhere.

Lord, for years I have been dying
Leeched white by sterile days,
Lacklustre nights; instead of trying
To exorcise the haze
Of tepid piety – instead of crying
Out for grace, I mouthed your praise

While desperate to feel your fire in me,
Yet dreaded it, resisted till the kiss
Of apathy
Or warm embrace of fickleness
Would welcome my return to the
Familiar chapel of my emptiness.

You could have driven me pure
Transfigured me with light – one vision
Just one! would have made me sure
This life of yours was really mine.
Each day, like a dog, I waited for
Your unmistakeable sign

And now it comes – as flaming blood
Distilling fear to keener fear
And no escape; no ark bobs on the flood
Of this fetid waveless atmosphere –
The dark age has come – God
Deliver me, prepare

My soul . . .
                the world's light darkens
The future tunnels to the past
This blank paper is my afterlife, a token
Of the hope I've lost.
Lord start again. Make the earth
Afresh from this

                Great Dearth

Cranborne Woods (17 May 1994)

IN MEMORY OF MY MOTHER

We stopped the car, ducked below the fence
Felt time unravelling in a revelation
The seconds fall and scatter into thousands

Of tiny saints, a reborn multitude
Flowing past the trees, through pools of sun,
Each earthly form a spirit flame, pure blue.

They watched us drift among them, large as gods,
As if we'd come as part of their parousia
To stay with them forever in these woods.

As time grew darker we slipped away like ghosts
And slowly drove . . . towards your death next May
When once again I saw the risen host

Could watch you walking weightlessly among
The welcomers, the gently swaying throng.

Look here I am in various parts –
In whole I'm found in all the starts –
God made me one so you may ask
How I'm the sunset, coloured glass
The comet and the shooting star.

[*see pages 52–3*]

Also by James Harpur

The Monk's Dream

'James Harpur's second book is disciplined, intelligent and repays several readings... His sources are the Bible, the *Aeneid*, Bede and Irish laments. But Harpur doesn't flirt with erudition. *The Monk's Dream* is an intricate exploration of death – not death alone, but the mystery that surrounds the experience... The title poem... suggests a belief in unseen forces, be they supernatural or imaginative; because of these, an ordinary life is significant beyond death. This idea also informs several of the book's excellent translations and adaptations. In all, *The Monk's Dream* is a finely weighted and balanced work of elegy.'

RICHARD TYRELL, *Times Literary Supplement*

'His whole collection represents a struggle with a conundrum with mortality... At the centre is the sonnet sequence about his father's death, 'The Frame of Furnace Light'. It is an extraordinary piece of writing... Harpur represents his father with such clarity and sympathy as to render his gradual decline almost unbearable.'

MAGGIE O'FARRELL, *Poetry Review*

A Vision of Comets

'Harpur's tunes are chiefly lyrical... the "welter of accumulated memories" is skilfully caught.'

WILLIAM SCAMMELL, *Independent on Sunday*

'James Harpur's first collection [has] a sense of the sacred running in parallel to the quotidian, and while the poems often reach into the exotic or esoteric, they are nevertheless accurately and cleanly made observances of a world the senses have access to.'

MARY RYAN, *Poetry Ireland Review*

'Harpur's sensibility is attuned to love, time, myth, the numinous – the makings of poetry... Harpur has an imaginative wonder.'

ANDREW WATERMAN, *London Magazine*

New and Recent Poetry from Anvil

Oliver Bernard
Verse &c.

Nina Bogin
The Winter Orchards

Nina Cassian
Take My Word for It

Martina Evans
All Alcoholics Are Charmers

Michael Hamburger
Intersections

Anthony Howell
Selected Poems

Marius Kociejowski
Music's Bride

Peter Levi
Viriditas

Gabriel Levin
Ostraca

Thomas McCarthy
Mr Dineen's Careful Parade

Stanley Moss
Asleep in the Garden

Dennis O'Driscoll
Weather Permitting

Peter Scupham
Night Watch

Daniel Weissbort
What Was All the Fuss About?